Mouth Quill
Poems with Ancestral Roots

Kaja Weeks

A Publication of The Poetry Box®

Poems ©2020 Kaja Weeks
All rights reserved.

Editing & Book Design by Shawn Aveningo Sanders
Cover Layout by Robert R. Sanders
Cover Photograph by Michael Huang
Author Photograph by Daniel Bottner

No part of this book may be reproduced in any manner whatsoever without permission from the author, except in the case of brief quotations embodied in critical essays, reviews and articles.

ISBN: 978-1-948461-62-7
Printed in the United States of America.
Wholesale Distribution via Ingram.

Published by The Poetry Box®, 2020
Portland, Oregon
ThePoetryBox.com

*Dedicated to my sister, Anu-Irja Ojamaa,
the memory of my brother, Tönu Parming
(Pärnu, Estonia, 1941 - Toronto, Canada, 1998),
and the memory of my brother,
Prüt Parming (Pärnu, Estonia, 1938 – Teaneck, NJ, 2019)*

and with love to

John, Aili, Jamison, and Elena Grace

The term "mouth quill" derives from suude sulg,
a poetic symbol for the singer's magical tool
found in Estonian runic verse:

Tooge mulle suude sulge . . . Siis mina laulan linnu keeli

Bring to me my mouth quill . . .
Then I shall sing in the voice of birds

Contents

Beneath Ice Sheets
Ancestral Journey — Beneath Ice Sheets   9
Little Songbird   10
Old Tunes on Spruce   11
Coastal Meadows   12
Midsummer Birches   13
Seabrook Farms (1949)   14
The Songstress (Pine Barrens, South Jersey)   16

The Milky Way
Ancestral Journey — The Milky Way   19
In the Whir of Wings   20
Gift for Curses   21
The Rise   22
The Horse and the Wolf   23
Swing Song   24
Red Berry (New Jersey, 1959)   25

Helix
The Dolomite Heel Print   29
Garden and Thicket   34
Mouth Quill   36
Gathering Grandmother Miili   37
Salme-in-Silk   39
Voices (Song Festival, Tallinn, Estonia)   40
Ancestral Journey — Helix   41

Notes   42

Acknowledgments	45
Praise for *Mouth Quill*	46
About the Author	49
About The Poetry Box®	50

Beneath Ice Sheets

Ancestral Journey — Beneath Ice Sheets

My ancestors migrated forward in time,
but I migrate backward —

back to the Baltic Ice Lake, melting,
overflowing with spectacular rivers of waterfalls.

Through a chink in cosmic space,
I enter, dive below refrozen melt.

Beneath ice sheets, lies land mother will call home,
and I will plummet to find my origins.

My imagination lacks the capacity
to go back as far as the Silurian time,

when this northland lay at the equator,
before everything broke and shifted,

though it flows through my dreams
like annihilation at the edge of time.

I will anchor to these instead:

    Saaremaa island will emerge from a crystalline basin,
        crushed remnants of sea life
        adhering to her granite cliffs.

    Pärnu will appear like a miracle on a bay,
        sail-way to *Saaremaa* by summer,
        ice-crossings, meters-deep, by winter.

    Just south, *Lüvimaa*'s thawed sea waves
        will scatter amber
        at our ancestor's feet.

Little Songbird

Mareta's melodies,
old Vaike's visions —
all these I carried,
fragments and whole.

Lives conjured into air
by sounds that never stop,
murmured into history
from cradle to bier —

those runic tunes
of lost silver beads,
snakes, rain charms
and northern stars.

When darkness descended
too early
and too full —
I sang, took flight.

Old Tunes on Spruce

My foremothers cradled
harps of northern spruce
in their laps—their strings
form my birth-ribs,

from which plucked-tones rise,
cluster and peal.
Drawing air to breathe,
I taste evergreen.

I am a spring twig, just six.
My melody slips its bent-tone
below the peak of a modal scale,
hinting at heartbreak.

But by twelve, cattle-train wheels
on Siberian metal haunt me.
Their din vanquishes lyric sound,
splitting my chest's veneer.

Yet, unbidden, vocal cords quiver,
resonate—steal space in my bony frame.
Ah, I see, it's not my space, but ancestral,
where bird-warbles became runic songs—

Kukukuu, pillilill, vaak vaak vaa . . .
Spirits seize me,
wounded *kannel*-wood sweats amber—
pulls me, holds me in primeval sap.

Coastal Meadows

The coastal meadows blaze golden,
break blue water, blue sky.
A wooden boat nudges
through green and purple marsh reeds.

Instantly, I am home.
I have never been here, but this place
settles me—the grassland cradling,
as if singing and rocking an infant to sleep.

Who slipped this place in me?
Was it my choosing, or has it crept unknown?
When did it come to quicken my breath
and then supply a resting sigh?

I am a refugee's child—
daughter of a true native daughter
of southwestern Estonia—who grew
with her mother's hollow in her heart.

I long for the resting sigh she was ripped from,
for the sway of reed plumes on her seaward creek.
Her stories, a mirage of sounds, and my yearning—
gild sight, bending time and space.

Midsummer Birches

Jaaniöö birch leaves bitter-sweeten the air.
A young man's beloved rides his silk-tufted horse.
Kaasike, kaasike, the refrain sounds.
Trot with pride, mane bedecked with bangles!

The girl's limbs are solstice-bare —
she aches for birch-scented infusion.
If not on this night graced by radiance
when light eclipses dark, then when?

Beyond the forest's edge bonfires burn,
wood crackles, fire-snaps leap high.
To distant singing she intones her *runo*,
the mythic fern-blossom shines.

Rain's tiny, cool watery jewels
form a sloppy necklace above her collarbone.
Silver baubles with no lacing, they break,
spill one after another, slip down her torso.

Birch essence vanished,
pearled rain has taken her down.
Upon dark moss beneath white branches, she wears
these glistening gems not with conceit, but surrender.

Seabrook Farms
(1949)

I retrace your shell-shocked footsteps into the New World,
but neither prints nor scents endure.

Pungent winds wrinkle vast fields—
spinach, peas and corn—
Jersey farmland that absorbed you
into their united essence.

Like crops squatting in neat, long rows
wooden barracks form Hoover Village,
where I see you caught in the alley
by brutal winds—

a pale blue uniform
flailing from your waist.
A deep tritone whistle blows,
harbinger of a ten-hour night-shift ahead.

You trudge with others,
those who fled with you
from a landscape riven by flames
into the stormy Baltic Sea—

the world gone mad with war once more:
forced German labor in exchange
for cheating certain Russian death,
five years in displaced persons camp limbo,

till the blustery voyage on a U.S. Navy ship;
then, hauled on the back of Charles F. Seabrook's
open farm truck to this rural company town—
You mumble, *home*, until it rises like a question.

I plant my future-self in your path
but can't feel you pass through.
Please—I can't even be a shadow
if I have no object.

Not yet born to cruelty or compassion,
I don't care that you stand twelve hours
at the conveyor belt, falling from exhaustion.
I don't care how senselessly

daze shimmers in your eyes.
I will stay and cavort
inside your stunned mind
until you can wake to yourself,

but do not fear, Mother—
we are not alone:
your starched white hat bobs along
with resettled Nisei ladies',

sorting peas for freezing,
field-raked by Tennessee migrants,
Estonian boys, West Indies laborers,
former German prisoners of war —

a motley crew of the dispossessed,
stitched into a patchwork of America.

The Songstress
(Pine Barrens, South Jersey)

~ In Memory of Ellen Parve Valdsaar

Magical songstress,
dressed in linen,
a woven, currant-white belt
wrapped three times
around her waist —
the long end falling freely.

In darkness
she stood alone,
spot-lit in a field.
We waited, almost in silence,
except for those summer night-sounds —
crickets, a branch-crackle, bullfrogs.

When she opened her mouth
and high sounds emerged,
they were fantastical —
glides and leaps upon vowels,
singing, whistling or bird song.
Some were shepherd's calls, *Aaaae, aaae!*

Murueide tütred came —
those sprites, whose singing drove
animals of the forest to thrive.
Mythic images of the yolk and white
of a bird's egg washed to shore —
our sun and moon — appeared.

The Milky Way

Ancestral Journey — The Milky Way

Over bog spirits and sacred groves,
our songs will enshrine air.
But first, in the vaults of time and space,
I will begin as the spirit of an egg,

carried by the sea to Iberia.
Here, I will land on a branch
of the daughters of Eve,
and their hunter gatherer men.

As the glacier melts,
plants sprout northward,
and we will move toward the Urals,
threading mountain edges,

tundra and colossal rivers.
Through a thousand summers and winters,
some will be left in river-bends,
some follow the reindeer north.

Some will look heavenward at traces of bird-flight,
some walk a milky star-path westward.
Dreams float through moonlit nights,
enter open windows,

land upon our sleepy brows:
Uni tule, uni tule lapse silma pääle.
Metrical pulses move our language,
first syllables drum the words,

forward, until we reach the sea — *Eesti.*

In the Whir of Wings

Mother is gone by dawn,
and will not be back until dark,
when I crouch by the window,
layers of drapes pulled round me.

Day is life, but life is in the hands
of the ruler of our universe.
Our space is dark, enclosed, silent,
but for the man's sudden sounds—

a barrage of words, a command,
his angry *Kurat*, the *r* quadrupling,
until it trills—*Kurrrrat!*
Devil! Damn!

So that my heart must beat in time
with that unbearable line of sounded fury,
to know when his hurled object will crash—
landing with the final spit *t* of *Kurrrrat*.

I need to fly like a bird
in mother's lullaby,
Püri, pääri pääsukene . . .
Püri, pääri, püri, pääri—

sounds like the whir of wings,
when the swallow flies,
one eye looking behind
to watch out for him.

Gift for Curses

The man had a gift for curses,
harvested from the old country.
Wickedness and hunger, knee to knee,
bred endless word-nettles —
so precise, so colorful, rich in meaning,
stealthily growing under his tongue,
ready to launch each sting
with perfect aim.

It only took sixty years to dull those paternal projectiles.
My sister and I nearly had a peaceful Thanksgiving,
as we laughingly tripped over the powerless dead man's
Vana pastla tald — You sole of an old sandal,
found ourselves doubled over with
Igavene tõbras — You everlasting beast,
hurled *Lambapea* and *Tainapea —*
Sheep's head and *Dough head* at each other.

But *Kuradi oinas — Goddamn ram* concussed us,
Kas ajud kivistanud? — Has your brain fossilized? petrified,
Ähmanud — Bleary, dim-witted, fogged us, and
the pall of *Näost loidunud — Stagnant-face,* nauseated.

Those images we still see
in dreams, stripped of laughs.
Our lips press tight, remembering —
he aimed most of those curses at Mother.

The Rise

Mother's lulled notes,
old whispers,
nuzzled my ear
on late nights.

I could hardly catch
their fuzzy edges
as sleep took me.
Äiu, äiu, kussu, kussu.

Mother's mother was born
on a farm near the sea—
Southern Estonia, 1895.
Sea-grey waves rustle,

sleep mists its way
from coastal stones
crosses a thousand miles,
falls upon my eye.

Song saved me. Like steam
from your smoke-sauna,
my spirits rose skyward,
hissing before the rise.

The Horse and the Wolf

Magic is enacted
over and over
in *Hobusemäng*.

Child-horses prance
and summon the wolf,
who breaks a horse's neck.

The children circle, run
and surrender all day—their cries,
a spell to keep real danger away.

Ollalii, Lellalii, Ollalii, Lellalii
is their call, delighted,
nonsensical, nearly maniacal.

Which is the horse who is taken?
She's flaxen-maned,
with a blaze.

I am the horse
with flaxen hair,
my face a-blaze,

Catch me now!

In nightmares,
I still holler to you,
the wolf.

Why do I call you?
Because, once,
you broke my neck.

I cross my fingers—chant,
Ollalii, Lellalii, Ollalii, Lellalii

Swing Song

Wind blows white blond hair,
combed cotton, soft on my neck.

Kügele... Ae, ae

Sunlight drizzles through leaves
on the tall swing my brother built.

What do you see, my sister, just four?
Arc, move higher, over the treetops.

Kügele... Ae, ae

Behind the boulder, the sack-man,
who slings me into bags shifts shape, I say.

My shoes point up, my head down,
curled over pine board, I hover, grip ropes.

Kügele... Ae, ae

I am two girls, now I am three.
Swing, can you hold us all?

Push me higher than the sky,
Push me higher, faster, boost me,

Kügele... Ae, ae

into the cloud boat, my brother, dear

Ae ae ae ae, ae ae ae ae

Red Berry
(New Jersey, 1959)

Mother, I see no crossroad, no rock mossed
with softest threads, no signs of sacred space.

Still, I hope you will carry me there,
for a cosmic explosion fell upon our yard, too.

On *Saaremaa, Kaali's* plume cracked glass spherules
into fiery air and onto the ground, spilled hot snow.

Its crater became a lake, laden with ritual sacrifices—
while, here, our cataclysm created invisible ruin.

But we're just like those ancient un-dead,
our eyes open, awaiting the next terrible strike.

On your knees, you till hardpan earth
until eggshells, used coffee-grinds,

and your own eye-water yield loam.
Against all odds, buds form.

Let me put this red berry on your garden stones.
Take my offering, hear my cry.

Helix

The Dolomite Heel Print

I.

When I tell you about my visit,
I will not tell of *Pärnu* Bay;
How her pale midnight sun
casts a gold wash
of lacy ginger fronds
on empty, swaying swings that rise
from silken sand so soft
it swallows your feet.

Or how shell-pink luminous clouds gather
into their low blousons endless sea and dunes;
how the breeze shimmies your bare thighs
and shivers up your back, caresses your neck,
blows gauzy hair over your eyes;
how you could walk forever on the white sand
straight into the sea—how when you turn around,
your footprints will be gone.

II.

For you, my *pagulas* sister,
I will unravel the mystery
of chalky boot prints
that stained the land;
of white, grey-veined minerals
bound to blood, tamped into soil
by footfalls that will
never be gone.

III.

Just a sail from *Pärnu* Bay is *Saaremaa*,
isle of orchids, long-necked cranes,
windmills and ancient limestone.
Once, from their bedrock, islanders were forced
to quarry dolomite for Teutonic Crusaders,
for an oppressor-Bishop's fortress.
Majestic and unique, *Kuressaare* Castle
survives and still faces the sea intact.

Here, murmurs seem to rise from moats,
whip round medieval dolomite pillars—
they suffuse the wind.
No, listen, they carry the howls of 1941—
of Stalin's conquering soldiers,
who left island corpses under mounds,
in cellars, under stones, in the well,
ghosts in the fortress courtyard.

A cobbler, fishermen, children,
the lady who cares for old folks.
Women's breasts wrapped with barbed wire.
Those limed in layers to decompose.
Those mutilated genderless.
Those boiled alive in retribution.
The rest, too barbaric to say.

Ask instead, if you dare, after
Okinawans jumping
from murderous cliffs to killing waters.

IV.

Remember, my *pagulas* sister?

> That foul rumble of war—our people's refugee-years,
> fleeing charred land they'd never regain.
> Mothers abandoned on farms, brothers shot for resisting,
> uncles on cattle trains bound for Siberian gulags.
> On the run—children curled under benches,
> sneaking into haylofts or sleeping in graveyards.

Remember, my *pagulas* sister?

> All that before our births, yet rioting through our veins.
> We were spared, yet free to be expat *Kungla* bards,
> honor-guard-lasses upholding the lost republic's flag.
> But inside, blue from fear, as true-congregant-elders
> peered through us, like glass girls—
> our sacrifices too small.

Remember, my *pagulas* sister?

> In 1970, *Öö Pime* was smuggled from Estonia
> and we sang it, hymn-like, for *Maarjamaa pind*, holy land;
> sang of *lubjavildi kand*, unknowing what that was.
> Don't ask how we sustained breath while we wept inwardly
> for ancestral lands never imprinted by our feet,
> or how its acrid air wafted into our waking dreams.

Ask instead, if you dare, how wind endures
blowing through Cambodian killing fields,
or how anyone endures after tragedy.

V.

If you ask of that *lubjavildi kand*,
I will describe dolomite in Saaremaa's bedrock: limestone.
Traces of primeval mud, iron and sea fossils
now a timeless emblem as Estonia's national stone.

VI.

Öö Pime, Öö Pime,
Dark night.
I didn't know.
I know too much:
children's skeletons under Estonian soil
while island orchids still grew,
waves washing over fissures of ancient karst,
grey sediment immured in bloody prints.

But in summer 1941, Russian troops surged onto that ground—
in their absurd soft boots, and the mystery of their print
revealed to me at Saaremaa castle, by the man, raised as a boy
in the shadow of its howls, while we grew in America.

When the conquering regiments arrived
they wore boots not of leather but of plain felt.
Cheap, no match for the elements.
What fortified those Russian soldier's boots?

Dolomite—soaked into the felt, then let dry.
But, eventually, the dolomite leached
onto the land, and those chalky heel prints—
lubjavildi kand—left in their wake.

The man's face is pale now, my eyes dark holes.
No, I will not see, I want to say,
knowing we both watch ghosts rise from limed corpses
beneath the ground upon which we stand.

Ask no more of prints, of others' dolomite heels, or our own.
To a blue-veined, glass girl crushed with ancestral *klint*,
pulsing with murmurs and howls,
they are all unfathomable —

as mind-splitting as Chibok girls abducted to thorny forests,
or Rohingya, drowning in the Sea of Bengal.

VII.

But let me tell you
of *Pärnu* Bay in midsummer
when sun glows sand gold
and washes your forehead,
cheeks, mouth and eyelashes,
your warm bare shoulders and breasts.
Let me tell you of wind blowing cool spray
as you laugh and lean squinting into it.

Look for the lowest white cloud,
without ghosts.
Now, catch its sail!
We can surf endlessly, my friend,
south, toward *Kuramaa*
or slip past *Saaremaa*,
swirl deftly around the *Kattegatt*
and west to the open sea.

Surely, if we could look back,
our footprints would be gone.

Garden and Thicket

We always spoke pre-war Estonian,
though I emerged displaced in America.

How *kastetilgad—dewdrops* flowed
from your tongue, consonants curbed with breath.

Rändaja's high R trilled,
like a bird in flight, feathered *wanderer*.

Double vowels, a diphthong: *veeauru—vapor*,
slips through with one final floating sound.

I can sail all day on the waves of that,
then rest on *Mother—Ema's* murmur and hum.

Was this mother tongue your magic?
By three, I spoke your words—small amulets.

By five, I withdrew, the budding sounds
pressed against my chest to escape his scathing

segi paisatud—jumbled havoc, aimed at our faces,
his *Kuradi raisk!—Goddamned waste!* I still hear today.

My early words would re-emerge years later,
but I had to translate them for those who listened.

And who among them, including me, could grasp
the multitude of their meanings by then?

At midnight, my lips auto-form whispers.
I want to linger on soft diphthongs: *aiaõue—*

*into the garden—*blooming with songs
and memory I go, but these double vowels:

äärmuslikumates — in the extremity,
still lead to the thorn-clad thicket.

I can't escape this terrible beauty
that first began within the space

of your petals — folded up,
like a hibiscus at night.

Mouth Quill

At home, my stroke-assaulted mother,
you startle and confound me.
On my childhood bed
we eye each other.

Metallic sounds ring from your mouth.
Wailing not at gods, but from some crucible *of* the gods.
From those Northlands winds blow low and rise, they ripen.
Your incantation pelts the room, the color of blue sorrow—

one river, two rivers, three rivers, more . . .

My voice fails. I fear to go there and utter nothing.
I offer recorded purity, nuns singing 9th century Christian chant:
Gloria, laus, et honor tibi sit. Rex Christe, Redemptor.
Isn't this your God?

No! You smack the music device
and, though words have eluded you for months,
deep-throated, you decree, "This is false death!"
and renew your endless spell.

We are so far from singing together.
I don't know how to join you: my mouth quill has stilled.

Oh, *Mesi Marja-memmekene*, Honey Mama-berry,
Emakene hellekene, my Mother my dear.
Äiu, äiu, äiu, once you charmed me to slumber
on silken nets in this space of braided hair.

Gathering Grandmother Miili

At six, I only knew you by black dress
and serious face—a single armoire photo,
a sole relative to us in America,
your daughter's final refuge.

At eight, I heard your eyes were green,
just like my mother's—and mine.
I calmed, in the secret belief
this made the three of us soul mates.

After her wartime flight,
your eyes never met hers,
nor ever saw mine.
Did you know I existed?

At twelve, I collected your letters,
on airmail-thin, blue paper,
addressed to your daughter
with a coded identity.

Creeping up four flights of stairs
to a crammed office where
I murmured, *Maria Karro*—
not my mother's name.

After my mother was gone, I first saw
a letter in your rounded script
refer to *Little Kaja* and wept—
your endearment, half a century old.

I finally met you last summer in *Pärnu*,
in a lightly wooded cemetery by a river.
My husband spotted you, my son-in-law
scraped the stone that declared, "Miili."

My daughter and I planted white asters,
tilled with soil from America,
from your daughter's grave,
and I sang you a song.

Salme-in-Silk

Adapted from Tähemõrsja (Starbride).
In memory of my mother, Salme

On a field, moist with morning fog, by a craggy path,
a little hen's egg lay—no nest, poor thing, just dew.

A widow spied it, clutched the chilly shell,
then tucked the treasure into her apron pocket.

For three months and a day, she warmed the egg,
until the foundling, a girl, was born.

Salme bloomed—a maiden whom many courted,
wooed with gifts and sought to wed.

Not to the Sun with fifty horses,
nor to the waxing-then-waning moon,

but to a celestial suitor, steady and bright—
son of the North Star—she turned.

Hidden in time, I whispered: *Wed, Maid Salme, with Starry Youth,
so airy and silver-voiced, your daughter I will be.*

*The tall wise oaks and dashing alders, their trailing catkins, roots and branches,
all to your wedding who come, my uncles and aunties—my kin shall be.*

Salme-in-silk and Star-a-shimmering,
the Cross-Cane danced upon the green.

Thus betrothed, chariot alit,
they ascended to dwell in the sky.

Voices
(Song Festival, Tallinn, Estonia)

Song-Mother's voices
    Sounds of forebears once slipped from tongue to air,
    ribbon-like, still unfurling.

On the edge of the sea
    a silver shell holds thousands, singers who face
    thousands more on a grassy gentle rise. All inhale.

Though the hour nears midnight
    sun skims waters of the Baltic Sea,
    flames in the tower-torch leap high.

The singing will not stop,
    Lee — lee — lo, the sounds form *Leelo!*
    Each ancient syllable earned with sweat and love.

A conductor, peering from within a laurel wreath
    clasps his chest, lowers his head,
    bows to the choir who has honored song.

The watchers become the singers,
    the standing levitate,
    the air is alive.

Swirling round, melodies rustle, loosen hair,
    saying, we are a living sound — sing us speak us hear us.
    Song-Mother's voices — *Hääli imedänne!*

Ancestral Journey — Helix

Her name I cannot say,
she, who, on time's foggy sled,

began a journey
I will never know.

Once, a woman followed reindeer north
instead of the Milky Way west.

Once, a woman lived beneath Arctic light,
where night-greens and violet-blues quivered,

a woman whose line Mother drew to me,
with the pattern's shining segment, Saami!

Roots revealed to my daughter by DNA
in New York, the year, 2014.

Saami — Lappland, carried in a coded helix,
living heirs in spiral strands —

a legacy that unbinds, then re-roots.

Notes

Influences:

Ancient Estonian song verses (*runo/regi*) inspired my poems through their language, imagery and rhetorical devices. Specific poems: *Hobusemäng* (Horseplay), *Imekene Memmekene* (Mother dear), *Jaan tuli Jaanitulele, Jaanike* (Jaan came to the midsummer bonfire), *Karja hõiked, Helletused* (Shepherd's calls, Lullabies-Vocalises), *Küla mul ütleb* (The Village tells me), *Lähme Küke Katsumaie* (Let's go Swinging), *Lind Lohutamas* (The Bird's Consoling), *Loomine* (Creation), *Piiri-pääri Pääsukene* (Piiri-pääri Swallow), *Nägin Saaremaa Põlema* (I Saw Saaremaa on Fire), *Pill ol' Helle* (The Instrument was Sweet), *Tähemõrsja* (Starbride), *Veli, hellä vellekene* (Sweet Brother)

Veljo Tormis (1930-2017), songs, *Unustatud Rahvad* (Forgotten Peoples).

Lennart Meri (1929-2006), documentary films of Finno-Ugric migration: *Veelinnurahvas* (The Waterfowl People) and *Linnutee Tuuled* (The Winds of the Milky Way).

Estonian Terms Found in Poems:

"Ancestral Journey — Beneath Ice Sheets"
Pärnu – coastal town in southwest Estonia
Saaremaa – largest island off the southwest coast of Estonia
Lüvimaa – historical coastal region of southern Estonia, northern Latvia

"Old Tunes on Spruce"
Kannel – a zither, first played by the God of Music and Poetry
Kukukuu, pillilill – bird chatter in runic song verses

"Midsummer Birches"
Jaaniöö – midsummer's eve
Kaasike – call invoking a wedding singer
Runo – ancient Estonian song verses

"The Songstress (Pines Barrens, South Jersey)"
Murueide tütred - maidens of the Lady of Grass

"Ancestral Journey — The Milky Way"
Uni tule, uni tule lapse silma pääle – Sleep, come upon the child's eye, runic song verse
Eesti – Estonia

"In the Whir of Wings"
Püri, pääri – bird twitter
Pääsukene – swallow

"The Rise"
Äiu, äiu, kussu, kussu – lulling sounds in runic song verses

"The Horse and the Wolf"
Hobusemäng – horse play
Ollalii, Lellalii – a play call in Estonian runic song verses

"Swing Song"
Kügele – To the swing, a call in runic song verses
Ae – a call

"Red Berry"
Kaali – giant meteorite explosion upon Saaremaa island, Estonia, circa 1500 BC

"The Dolomite Heel Print"
Pagulas – refugee; here, those Estonians who fled during WWII
Kungla – a promised land in Estonian mythology
Öö Pime – Dark Night, a song

Maarjamaa Pind – Mary's Land, a poetic, reverential term for Estonia
Lubjavildi kand – dolomite heel print
Klint – ancient cracks in the earth's crust of Baltic coastal limestone cliffs
Kuramaa – coastal Latvian land with historic kinfolk ties to Saaremaa
Kategatt – Danish for "Cat's Throat," a strait connecting the Baltic and North seas

"Mouth Quill"
Mouth quill, *suude sulg*, is a singer's magic tool—found in runic song verses

"Voices"
Hääli imedänne – magical voices
Leelo – old word for song, and the title of an actual song

Acknowledgments

These poems, in earlier versions, first appeared in the following publications:

Bluestem Magazine: "Coastal Meadows"

Estonian World Global Magazine: "Voices (Tallinn, Estonia)"

Journal of Mythic Poetry and Fiction: "Salme-in-Silk" (as "The Wedding of Salme")

Sugar House Review: "Mouth Quill"

Special thanks to my long-time teachers and creative partners at New Directions, a writing program of The Washington-Baltimore Center for Psychoanalysis, and with gratitude to April Ossmann for her poetic and editorial guidance.

Praise for Mouth Quill

"I am a refugee's child . . . I long for the resting sigh she was ripped from . . ." writes Kaja Weeks in her poem "Coastal Meadows" from her collection, *Mouth Quill: Poems with Ancestral Roots*. Weeks's exploration of her Estonian heritage in twenty-one riveting poems swept me with her back to "those runic tunes of lost silver beads," then forward to her mother's escape as one of "a motley crew of the dispossessed/stitched into a patchwork of America." Rich with birds and melody, these pages sing, but her incredible "The Dolomite Heel Print" makes sure we understand not all songs are merry. Mouth Quill, a dark crystal studded with light, amazes.

—Deirdre Callanan, author of *Water~Dreaming* and *Fish Camp: North Jetty Tales*

Estonian runic verse inspires second-generation American poet Kaja Weeks' vivid lyric poems, beginning with the title, which refers to "the singer's magical tool," and aptly describes this poet's "quill" as well, delighting with wonderfully musical and evocative language: "Mother, I see no crossroad, no rock mossed/ with softest threads, no signs of sacred space."

We travel back in time to her parents' escape from a "world gone mad with war once more," to forging a diasporic post-WWII life, to her late mother's hospitalization, "Wailing not at gods, but from some crucible of the gods," to the poet's more recent adventures visiting her parents' homeland. Weeks' consideration of identity through the lens of history is visceral and heartfelt; and the inclusion of Estonian language and culture deft; as is the haunting intertwining of world history and family history; and the subject of immigration remains topical as ever, in the home of the Statue of Liberty.

—April Ossmann, author of *Event Boundaries*

Equally inspired by the traumatic geo-political history of Estonia, her ancestral land, and by the alliterative musicality of the Estonian language, Kaja Weeks has woven the archetypal story of conquered nations and displaced persons into a series of lyric poems that resonate with historical importance and quiver with delicate beauty. In poem after poem, Weeks uncovers the mythic imprint of an ancient, unvanquished culture that has retained a strong sense of itself and nurtured its citizens through longstanding traditions of folk song and choral singing. Like the Estonian ancestors who came before her, Weeks sings both to celebrate and resist. "I can't escape this terrible beauty," she writes. "Blooming with songs/ and memory, I go."

—Kate Daniels, author
In the Months of My Son's Recovery and *The Niobe Poems*

Mouth Quill—Poems with Ancestral Roots is a touching, gorgeously written collection—such patient, meditative themes, such lushly imagined writing. "The Dolomite Heel Print," in particular, is a breathtaking exploration of history and life and identity ... a stunning piece! The collection feels like a deep dive into identity—what binds us, what tears us apart, the ways that family can become home.

—Hala Alyan, author
The Twenty-Ninth Year and *Salt Houses*

In *Mouth Quill*, a remarkably evocative collection of poems, Kaja Weeks celebrates Finno-Ugric traditions of lyricism and the reverence of nature. The ancient runic roots of these traditions rarely get the attention that they deserve, and they are well-served here. It is a pleasure to read the poems aloud, feeling the rhythms with which they are instilled. The poems are both intensely personal and resonate with a universal voice.

Ancestral Journey—Beneath Ice Sheets, the first poem of the first section, also titled Beneath Ice Sheets starts "My ancestors migrated forward in time, but I migrate backward," and to my mind this is a key to all twenty-one poems. Weeks integrates standing in the present and looking to a past that has been handed down to her— not just reporting on what she's been told, but having experienced the stories for herself, takes us with her.

Salme-in-Silk, in the third section, Helix, dedicated to the author's mother, struck a particular chord with me, because I had the honor of knowing Salme in the Estonian-American community, and she was an extraordinary woman. But reading the poem, written in a mystical and lyric voice, it transcends the personal and delivers a rich visceral experience. I hope these poems are read by many and enjoyed by all who do.

—Tiina Aleman, Estonian translator
Shape of Time, poems by Doris Kareva

Using her quill to comprehend, imagine, burst free and sing, the poems of Kaja Weeks in *Mouth Quill* are a testament to the splendor and endurance of the human spirit. Out of the howls of war, out of curses, murmurs of stricken mothers, and cries of an ancient, trampled landscape has come a poet of such capacity that one is left gasping. From ancient runes and primeval mud of Estonia, she swallows the unendurable and transforms it into the harp song of her ancestresses. From ancestors who "lived beneath Arctic light/ where night-green and violet-blues quivered," Weeks tells us her foremothers "cradled harps of northern spruce." If they could hear the music of their daughter, they would weep. Read these poems and sail on sung waves of "murmur and hum." It is an honor to hold these majestic verses in one's hands.

—Sara Mansfield Taber, author
Born Under an Assumed Name:
The Memoir of a Cold War Spy's Daughter

About the Author

Kaja Weeks is a poet, essayist and classically trained singer whose writing contemplates music and healing as well as identity through multiple generations. She is the American born daughter of World War Two refugees from Estonia, a northern land on the Baltic Sea. Moved by the pain and beauty of its history, she also loves the alliterative sounds, mythic lore and world views in that ancient Finno-Ugric culture. Many of these motifs, found in thousands of runic verses and long preserved by oral transmission, come alive in Kaja's creative work. Her poems, especially, weave new strands with timeless, universal themes of ancestors, displacement, migration, longing, and one's sense of self and other.

Kaja was named a "little songbird" by the time she was five, singing hundreds of Estonian and English songs. Now she is also a clinic-based music educator in Maryland who engages young children with autism to their earliest communications with playful singing. Her ideas on development and early communicative musicality have been represented in trainings, lectures, keynote addresses and in scholarly journals in the United States and Canada.

Kaja is a graduate of New Directions, a three-year writing program of the Washington Baltimore Center for Psychoanalysis, where she studied with renowned writers in all genres as well as specialists in depth psychology. Kaja's literary writing has appeared in *The Sugar House Review*; *Ars Medica: A Journal of Medicine, The Arts and Humanities*; *Under the Gum Tree*; *The Sandy River Review*; *The Potomac Review* (nominee, Pushcart Prize) and elsewhere.

<lyricovertones.com>

About The Poetry Box®

The Poetry Box® is a boutique publishing company that enjoys providing a platform for both established and emerging poets to share their words with the world through beautiful printed books and chapbooks.

Feel free to visit the online bookstore (thePoetryBox.com), where you'll find more titles including:

Impossible Ledges by Dianne Avey

Bee Dance by Cathy Cain

Like the O in Hope by Jeanne Julian

Moroccan Holiday by Lauren Tivey

Shadow Man by Margaret Chula

A Long, Wide Stretch of Calm by Melanie Green

What She Was Wearing by Shawn Aveningo Sanders

The Very Rich Hours by Gregory Loselle

Between States of Matter by Sherry Rind

My Miscellaneous Muse by Ralph La Rosa

*The Kingdom of Bird*s by Joan Colby

*Just the Girl*s by Pamela R. Anderson-Bartholet

and more . . .

www.ingramcontent.com/pod-product-compliance
Lightning Source LLC
LaVergne TN
LVHW040202080526
838202LV00042B/3286